Editor
Karen Tam Froloff

Managing Editor
Karen J. Goldfluss, M.S. Ed.

Editor-in-Chief
Sharon Coan, M.S. Ed.

Cover Artist
Barb Lorseyedi

Art Coordinator
Kevin Barnes

Art Director
CJae Froshay

Imaging
James Edward Grace

Product Manager
Phil Garcia

Publishers
Rachelle Cracchiolo, M.S. Ed.
Mary Dupuy Smith, M.S. Ed.

Practice Makes Perfect

Multipl...

GRADE 3

Author

Robert Smith

Teacher Created Materials, Inc.
6421 Industry Way
Westminster, CA 92683
www.teachercreated.com

ISBN-0-7439-3321-4

©2002 Teacher Created Materials, Inc.
Reprinted, 2004
Made in U.S.A.

Table of Contents

Introduction 3
Practice 1: Using the Multiplication Chart 4
Practice 2: Multiplication as Repeated Addition 5
Practice 3: Multiplying by 0, 1, 2, and 5 6
Practice 4: Multiplying by 0, 1, 2, 5, and 10 7
Practice 5: Multiplying by 0, 1, 2, 3, 4, and 5 8
Practice 6: Multiplying by 6, 7, 8, and 9 9
Practice 7: Mixed Practice 10
Practice 8: Mixed Practice 11
Practice 9: Missing Factors 12
Practice 10: Multiplying by 11 and 12 13
Practice 11: Multiplying with Three Factors (Commutative Property) . . 14
Practice 12: One-digit Multipliers and Two-digit Multiplicands 15
Practice 13: One-digit Multipliers and Two-digit Multiplicands 16
Practice 14: One-digit Multipliers and Two-digit Multiplicands 17
Practice 15: Multiplying by 10 and Two-digit Multiplicands 18
Practice 16: Multiplying by Multiples of 10 and Two-digit Multiplicands . . 19
Practice 17: Multiplying by 10 and Three-digit Multiplicands 20
Practice 18: Multiplying by Multiples of 10 and Three-digit Multiplicands . . 21
Practice 19: Multiplying by Multiples of 10 with Three Factors (Associative Property) 22
Practice 20: Multiplying by 100 23
Practice 21: Multiplying by 1,000 24
Practice 22: Two-digit Multipliers (No Regrouping) 25
Practice 23: Two-digit Multipliers (No Regrouping) 26
Practice 24: One-digit Multipliers and Three-digit Multiplicands (Some Regrouping) 27
Practice 25: One-digit Multipliers and Three-digit Multiplicands (Regrouping) 28
Practice 26: One-digit Multipliers and Four-digit Multiplicands (Regrouping) 29
Practice 27: Two-digit Multipliers (Regrouping) 30
Practice 28: Two-digit Multipliers (Regrouping) 31
Practice 29: Two-digit Multipliers (Regrouping) 32
Practice 30: Two-digit Multipliers and Three-digit Multiplicands 33
Practice 31: Two-digit Multipliers and Three-digit Multiplicands 34
Practice 32: Simple Word Problems 35
Practice 33: Simple Word Problems 36
Practice 34: Using Multiplication to Find the Area of Rectangles 37
Practice 35: Two-digit Multipliers and Four-digit Multiplicands 38
Practice 36: Three-digit Multipliers and Three-digit Multiplicands 39
Test Practice 1 40
Test Practice 2 41
Test Practice 3 42
Test Practice 4 43
Test Practice 5 44
Test Practice 6 45
Answer Sheet 46
Answer Key 47

ა ❂ ა ❂ ა Introduction ❂ ა ა ა ❂ ა

The old adage "practice makes perfect" can really hold true for your child and his or her education. The more practice your child has with concepts being taught in school, the more success he or she is likely to find. For many parents, knowing how to help their children can be frustrating because the resources may not be readily available.

As a parent it is also difficult to know where to focus your efforts so that the extra practice your child receives at home supports what he or she is learning in school.

This book has been designed to help parents and teachers reinforce basic skills with their children. *Practice Makes Perfect* reviews basic math skills for children in grade 3. The main focus is on multiplication. While it would be impossible to include in this book all concepts taught in grade 3, the following basic objectives are reinforced through practice exercises. These objectives support math standards established on a district, state, or national level. (Refer to the Table of Contents for the specific objectives of each practice page.)

- multiplication as repeated addition
- multiplication by 0, 1, 2, 3, 4, 5, 6, 7, 8, 9, 10, 11, and 12
- identifying missing factors
- multiplying with three factors
- multiplying with one-digit multipliers and two-digit multiplicands
- multiplying by 10 and multiples of 10, using two- and three-digit multiplicands

- multiplying with one-digit and two-digit multipliers, with and without regrouping
- using multiplication in simple word problems
- using multiplication to find the area of rectangles
- multiplying with three-digit multipliers and three-digit multiplicands
- multiplying with one-digit and two-digit multipliers and four-digit multiplicands

There are 36 practice pages organized sequentially, so children can build their knowledge from more basic to higher-level math skills. Following the practice pages are six test practices. These provide children with multiple choice test items to help prepare them for standardized tests administered in schools. As your child completes each test, he or she should fill in the correct bubbles on the answer sheet (page 46). To correct the test pages and the practice pages in this book, use the answer key provided on pages 47 and 48.

How to Make the Most of This Book

Here are some useful ideas for optimizing the practice pages in this book:

- Set aside a specific place in your home to work on the practice pages.
- Set up a certain time of day to work on the practice pages. This will establish consistency. An alternative is to look for times in your day or week that are less hectic and more conducive to practicing skills.
- Keep all practice sessions with your child positive and constructive. If the mood becomes tense, or you and your child are frustrated, set the book aside and look for another time to practice with your child.
- Help with instructions, if necessary. If your child is having difficulty understanding what to do or work the some problems through with him or her.
- Review the work your child has done. This serves as reinforcement and checks understanding.
- Allow your child to use whatever writing instruments he or she prefers. For example, colored pencils can add variety and pleasure to drill work.
- Pay attention to the areas in which your child has the most difficulty. Provide extra guidance and exercises in those areas. Allowing children to use drawings and manipulatives, such as coins, tiles, game markers, or flash cards, can help them grasp difficult concepts more easily.
- Look for ways to make real-life application to the skills being reinforced.

Practice 1

The multiplication chart shown here can be used to find any basic multiplication fact until you have learned them all.

One of the best ways to learn the facts is to practice using the chart.

Columns (Read Down)

Rows	1	2	3	4	5	6	7	8	9	10	11	12
1	1	2	3	4	5	6	7	8	9	10	11	12
2	2	4	6	8	10	12	14	16	18	20	22	24
3	3	6	9	12	15	18	21	24	27	30	33	36
4	4	8	12	16	20	24	28	32	36	40	44	48
5	5	10	15	20	25	30	35	40	45	50	55	60
6	6	12	18	24	30	36	42	48	54	60	66	72
7	7	14	21	28	35	42	49	56	63	70	77	84
8	8	16	24	32	40	48	56	64	72	80	88	96
9	9	18	27	36	45	54	63	72	81	90	99	108
10	10	20	30	40	50	60	70	80	90	100	110	120
11	11	22	33	44	55	66	77	88	99	110	121	132
12	12	24	36	48	60	72	84	96	108	120	132	144

Read **down** for the **Columns**.

Read **across** for the **Rows**.

Note: To find 7 times 9, run one finger down the 7 column and a finger on the other hand across the 9 row until they meet. The answer is the number 63 where the row and column intersect (meet).

Directions: Use the chart to do these problems.

1.   7
   x 9
	2. 5
	   x 4
		3. 9
		   x 3
			4. 6
			   x 2

5.   4
   x 4
	6. 5
	   x 5
		7. 6
		   x 6
			8. 3
			   x 3

Practice 2

Directions: Add each of these problems. Look for the pattern.

1. 5
   5
  + 5

2. 4
   4
  + 4

3. 2
   2
   2
  + 2

4. 6
   6
   6
  + 6

5. 8 + 8 + 8 = _____

6. 9 + 9 + 9 + 9 = _____

7. 2
   2
   2
   2
  + 2

8. 3
   3
   3
   3
   3
  + 3

9. 1
   1
   1
   1
   1
   1
  + 1

10. 7
   7
   7
   7
  + 7

11. 4 + 4 + 4 + 4 + 4 = _____

12. 3 + 3 + 3 + 3 + 3 = _____

13. 6
   6
   6
   6
  + 6

14. 5
   5
   5
   5
   5
  + 5

15. 9
   9
  + 9

16. 8
   8
   8
  + 8

Practice 3

Directions: Do these problems. Use your multiplication chart if you need help.

1. 1 x 1	**2.** 2 x 2	**3.** 5 x 2	**4.** 0 x 5	**5.** 2 x 5
6. 1 x 2	**7.** 0 x 1	**8.** 5 x 0	**9.** 2 x 0	**10.** 1 x 5
11. 2 x 0	**12.** 2 x 1	**13.** 6 x 1	**14.** 7 x 1	**15.** 9 x 1
16. 8 x 1	**17.** 4 x 0	**18.** 9 x 0	**19.** 6 x 0	**20.** 7 x 0
21. 9 x 2	**22.** 6 x 2	**23.** 7 x 2	**24.** 4 x 2	**25.** 7 x 5

Practice 4

Directions: Do these problems. Use your multiplication chart if you need help.

1. 9 x 1	**2.** 2 x 5	**3.** 9 x 2	**4.** 8 x 0	**5.** 8 x 2
6. 6 x 5	**7.** 9 x 1	**8.** 6 x 5	**9.** 8 x 5	**10.** 10 x 1
11. 5 x 0	**12.** 8 x 1	**13.** 7 x 2	**14.** 7 x 1	**15.** 10 x 2
16. 9 x 0	**17.** 4 x 0	**18.** 10 x 5	**19.** 8 x 0	**20.** 5 x 0
21. 4 x 5	**22.** 6 x 5	**23.** 8 x 5	**24.** 9 x 5	**25.** 0 x 0

Practice 5   ⟋ 🐚 ⟋ 🐚 ⟋ 🐚 ⟋ 🐚 ⟋ 🐚 ⟋ 🐚 ⟋ ⟋ 🐚

Directions: Do these problems. Use your multiplication chart if you need help.

1. 5 $\times 4$	**2.** 4 $\times 2$	**3.** 6 $\times 5$	**4.** 3 $\times 1$	**5.** 7 $\times 1$
6. 7 $\times 3$	**7.** 10 $\times 3$	**8.** 5 $\times 0$	**9.** 5 $\times 1$	**10.** 9 $\times 1$
11. 6 $\times 3$	**12.** 7 $\times 0$	**13.** 10 $\times 4$	**14.** 9 $\times 3$	**15.** 1 $\times 4$
16. 8 $\times 3$	**17.** 10 $\times 5$	**18.** 9 $\times 4$	**19.** 4 $\times 3$	**20.** 6 $\times 3$
21. 7 $\times 3$	**22.** 2 $\times 3$	**23.** 10 $\times 3$	**24.** 7 $\times 2$	**25.** 8 $\times 2$

Practice 6

Directions: Do these problems. Use your multiplication chart if you need help.

1.	3	2.	2	3.	4	4.	5	5.	5
	x 8		x 8		x 8		x 8		x 7

6.	1	7.	10	8.	4	9.	2	10.	4
	x 7		x 7		x 7		x 6		x 6

11.	3	12.	5	13.	5	14.	0	15.	2
	x 6		x 6		x 9		x 9		x 9

16.	1	17.	2	18.	5	19.	10	20.	7
	x 9		x 9		x 8		x 6		x 6

21.	5	22.	9	23.	7	24.	6	25.	7
	x 6		x 8		x 9		x 9		x 7

Practice 7 ◑ ◐ ◑ ◐ ◑ ◐ ◑ ◐ ◑ ◐ ◑ ◐ ◐ ◐

Directions: Do these problems. Use your multiplication chart, if needed.

1. 9 x 4	**2.** 7 x 6	**3.** 4 x 4	**4.** 0 x 9	**5.** 5 x 7
6. 9 x 8	**7.** 7 x 8	**8.** 6 x 1	**9.** 4 x 6	**10.** 10 x 4
11. 5 x 4	**12.** 3 x 8	**13.** 5 x 9	**14.** 8 x 8	**15.** 10 x 9
16. 5 x 8	**17.** 3 x 7	**18.** 9 x 7	**19.** 8 x 7	**20.** 6 x 8
21. 5 x 8	**22.** 9 x 10	**23.** 7 x 10	**24.** 6 x 1	**25.** 8 x 10

Practice 8

Directions: Do these problems. Use your multiplication chart, if needed.

1. 9
   x 8

2. 4
   x 9

3. 9
   x 7

4. 10
   x 6

5. 10
   x 4

6. 5
   x 0

7. 9
   x 3

8. 7
   x 1

9. 7
   x 7

10. 3
    x 10

11. 6
    x 9

12. 8
    x 7

13. 7
    x 9

14. 9
    x 5

15. 5
    x 7

16. 4
    x 7

17. 0
    x 10

18. 2
    x 9

19. 8
    x 4

20. 1
    x 6

21. 8
    x 6

22. 5
    x 2

23. 3
    x 0

24. 8
    x 9

25. 4
    x 7

Practice 9

Directions: Fill in the missing factors. Use your multiplication chart, if needed.

1.   10 x _____ = 50

2.   9 x _____ = 18

3.   5 x _____ = 20

4.   5 x _____ = 40

5.   _____ x 8 = 80

6.   7 x _____ = 35

7.   6 x _____ = 36

8.   8 x _____ = 32

9.   _____ x 6 = 60

10.   _____ x 7 = 42

11.   _____ x 9 = 81

12.   4 x _____ = 12

13.   2 x _____ = 18

14.   _____ x 7 = 49

15.   _____ x 8 = 48

16.   _____ x 6 = 48

17.   10 x _____ = 40

18.   9 x _____ = 72

19.   3 x _____ = 27

20.   6 x _____ = 24

21.   _____ x 5 = 50

22.   8 x _____ = 56

23.   _____ x 9 = 54

24.   6 x _____ = 54

25.   _____ x 3 = 21

26.   7 x _____ = 56

27.   _____ x 9 = 36

Practice 10

Directions: Do these problems. Use your multiplication chart, if needed.

1. 11 x 10	**2.** 12 x 10	**3.** 8 x 12	**4.** 11 x 12	**5.** 11 x 9
6. 11 x 3	**7.** 9 x 11	**8.** 6 x 12	**9.** 10 x 12	**10.** 9 x 12
11. 6 x 11	**12.** 4 x 12	**13.** 12 x 9	**14.** 11 x 8	**15.** 5 x 12
16. 7 x 11	**17.** 3 x 12	**18.** 12 x 11	**19.** 7 x 12	**20.** 4 x 12
21. 8 x 11	**22.** 5 x 11	**23.** 3 x 12	**24.** 8 x 12	**25.** 9 x 12

Practice 11

Directions: Compute the answer to each problem by multiplying any two of the factors. Then multiply that product by the third factor. The first one is done for you.

1. 2 x 4 x 3 =
    2 x 4 = 8
    8 x 3 = 24
    Answer: 24

2. 3 x 4 x 2 =
    3 x 4 = ____
    12 x 2 = ____
    Answer: ____

3. 4 x 2 x 3 =
    4 x 2 = ____
    8 x 3 = ____
    Answer:____

4. 3 x 6 x 2 =

    Answer:____

5. 6 x 2 x 3 =

    Answer:____

6. 2 x 3 x 6 =

    Answer:____

7. 5 x 6 x 4 =

    Answer:____

8. 6 x 5 x 4 =

    Answer:____

9. 4 x 5 x 6 =

    Answer:____

10. 7 x 3 x 5 =

    Answer:____

11. 3 x 5 x 7 =

    Answer:____

12. 5 x 7 x 3 =

    Answer:____

13. 9 x 4 x 2 =

    Answer:____

14. 4 x 2 x 9 =

    Answer:____

15. 2 x 9 x 4 =

    Answer:____

Practice 12

Directions: Do these problems. Use your multiplication chart, if needed. The first one has been done for you.

1. 12 x 4 48	**2.** 14 x 2	**3.** 13 x 3	**4.** 21 x 3	**5.** 21 x 6
6. 44 x 2	**7.** 22 x 4	**8.** 34 x 2	**9.** 50 x 8	**10.** 42 x 4
11. 54 x 2	**12.** 43 x 2	**13.** 33 x 3	**14.** 71 x 9	**15.** 67 x 1
16. 93 x 3	**17.** 45 x 2	**18.** 85 x 2	**19.** 35 x 4	**20.** 65 x 4
21. 70 x 9	**22.** 90 x 7	**23.** 50 x 6	**24.** 60 x 8	**25.** 32 x 5

Practice 13

Directions: Do these problems. Use your multiplication chart, if needed. The first one has been done for you.

1. 33
   x 3
   99

2. 15
   x 2

3. 23
   x 3

4. 41
   x 6

5. 51
   x 5

6. 34
   x 2

7. 25
   x 3

8. 32
   x 4

9. 25
   x 5

10. 23
    x 3

11. 24
    x 2

12. 22
    x 5

13. 18
    x 5

14. 27
    x 5

15. 36
    x 5

16. 36
    x 3

17. 44
    x 5

18. 33
    x 8

19. 66
    x 2

20. 55
    x 4

21. 34
    x 6

22. 37
    x 4

23. 28
    x 4

24. 65
    x 5

25. 26
    x 8

Practice 14

Directions: Do these problems. Use your multiplication chart, if needed. The first one has been done for you.

1. 63
   x 4
   252

2. 75
   x 6

3. 93
   x 7

4. 47
   x 6

5. 59
   x 5

6. 95
   x 8

7. 87
   x 5

8. 79
   x 3

9. 85
   x 7

10. 73
    x 7

11. 67
    x 9

12. 92
    x 4

13. 78
    x 9

14. 99
    x 8

15. 98
    x 7

16. 57
    x 8

17. 33
    x 7

18. 19
    x 3

19. 56
    x 7

20. 73
    x 9

21. 58
    x 9

22. 37
    x 6

23. 72
    x 9

24. 29
    x 8

25. 76
    x 8

Practice 15

Directions: Do these problems. Use your multiplication chart, if needed.

1. 12 x 10	**2.** 15 x 10	**3.** 23 x 10	**4.** 11 x 10	**5.** 22 x 10
6. 14 x 10	**7.** 33 x 10	**8.** 18 x 10	**9.** 20 x 10	**10.** 40 x 10
11. 30 x 10	**12.** 70 x 10	**13.** 24 x 10	**14.** 31 x 10	**15.** 62 x 10
16. 43 x 10	**17.** 44 x 10	**18.** 25 x 10	**19.** 37 x 10	**20.** 62 x 10

Practice 16 ⟳ ⟳ ⟳ ⟳ ⟳ ⟳ ⟳ ⟳ ⟳ ⟳ ⟳ ⟳ ⟳

Directions: Do these problems. Use your multiplication chart, if needed.

1. 32 x 20	**2.** 25 x 40	**3.** 13 x 30	**4.** 16 x 20	**5.** 15 x 30

6. 92 x 40	**7.** 17 x 50	**8.** 28 x 60	**9.** 23 x 30	**10.** 48 x 70

11. 18 x 80	**12.** 34 x 50	**13.** 21 x 20	**14.** 11 x 90	**15.** 54 x 40

16. 56 x 30	**17.** 55 x 50	**18.** 99 x 90	**19.** 33 x 30	**20.** 66 x 60

Practice 17 ⟋ ❧ ⟋ ❧ ⟋ ❧ ⟋ ❧ ⟋ ❧ ⟋ ❧ ⟋ ❧

Directions: Do these problems. Use your multiplication chart, if needed. The first two have been done for you.

1. 123
    x 10
    1,230

2. 543
    x 10
    5,430

3. 243
    x 10

4. 341
    x 10

5. 244
    x 10

6. 534
    x 10

7. 333
    x 10

8. 762
    x 10

9. 300
    x 10

10. 400
    x 10

11. 700
    x 10

12. 900
    x 10

13. 250
    x 10

14. 460
    x 10

15. 620
    x 10

16. 490
    x 10

17. 474
    x 10

18. 716
    x 10

19. 642
    x 10

20. 919
    x 10

Practice 18

Directions: Do these problems. Use your multiplication chart, if needed. The first one has been done for you.

1. 134 x 20 2,680	**2.** 711 x 50	**3.** 123 x 30	**4.** 145 x 40	**5.** 125 x 30

6. 342 x 20	**7.** 347 x 40	**8.** 221 x 40	**9.** 333 x 30	**10.** 444 x 40

11. 222 x 20	**12.** 111 x 90	**13.** 731 x 50	**14.** 604 x 90	**15.** 940 x 70

16. 472 x 70	**17.** 700 x 70	**18.** 500 x 40	**19.** 800 x 70	**20.** 300 x 80

Practice 19

Directions: Compute the answer to each problem by multiplying two of the factors. Then multiply that product by the third factor. The first one has been done for you.

1. 20 x 10 x 30 =
    20 x 10 = 200
    200 x 30 = 6,000
    Answer: 6,000

7. 80 x 90 x 20 =
    _____
    _____
    Answer: _____

2. 30 x 20 x 10 =
    30 x 20 = _____
    600 x 10 = _____
    Answer: _____

8. 70 x 80 x 40 =
    _____
    _____
    Answer: _____

3. 40 x 20 x 30 =
    40 x 20 = _____
    _____
    Answer: _____

9. 60 x 60 x 60 =
    _____
    _____
    Answer: _____

4. 70 x 20 x 10 =
    70 x 20 = _____
    _____
    Answer: _____

10. 40 x 40 x 40 =
    _____
    _____
    Answer: _____

5. 60 x 50 x 20 =
    _____
    _____
    Answer: _____

11. 90 x 80 x 70 =
    _____
    _____
    Answer: _____

6. 50 x 40 x 30 =
    _____
    _____
    Answer: _____

12. 20 x 40 x 60 =
    _____
    _____
    Answer: _____

Practice 20 ⊙ ⊙ ⊙ ⊙ ⊙ ⊙ ⊙ ⊙ ⊙ ⊙ ⊙ ⊙ ⊙ ⊙ ⊙

Directions: Do these problems. Use your multiplication chart, if needed. The first one has been done for you.

1. 23 x 100 2,300	**2.** 45 x 100	**3.** 19 x 100	**4.** 12 x 100	**5.** 42 x 100

6. 87 x 100	**7.** 33 x 100	**8.** 29 x 100	**9.** 400 x 100	**10.** 600 x 100

11. 300 x 100	**12.** 800 x 100	**13.** 712 x 100	**14.** 456 x 100	**15.** 817 x 100

16. 111 x 100	**17.** 438 x 100	**18.** 125 x 100	**19.** 982 x 100	**20.** 819 x 100

Practice 21 ⟳ ⟳ ⟳ ⟳ ⟳ ⟳ ⟳ ⟳ ⟳ ⟳ ⟳ ⟳ ⟳ ⟳

Directions: Do these problems. Use your multiplication chart, if needed. The first one has been done for you.

1. 14
    x 1000
    14,000

2. 21
    x 1000

3. 17
    x 1000

4. 28
    x 1000

5. 75
    x 1000

6. 33
    x 1000

7. 219
    x 1000

8. 495
    x 1000

9. 239
    x 1000

10. 200
    x 1000

11. 500
    x 1000

12. 400
    x 1000

13. 2345
    x 1000

14. 6126
    x 1000

15. 4949
    x 1000

16. 3498
    x 1000

Practice 22

Directions: Do these problems. Use your multiplication chart, if needed. The first one has been done for you.

1.
```
    12
  x 21
    12
 + 240
   252
```

2.
```
   14
 x 22
```

3.
```
   23
 x 12
```

4.
```
   31
 x 24
```

5.
```
   26
 x 11
```

6.
```
   34
 x 22
```

7.
```
   22
 x 32
```

8.
```
   13
 x 33
```

9.
```
   20
 x 57
```

10.
```
   40
 x 43
```

11.
```
   71
 x 62
```

12.
```
   43
 x 31
```

13.
```
   33
 x 22
```

14.
```
   41
 x 43
```

15.
```
   68
 x 11
```

16.
```
   23
 x 32
```

17.
```
   44
 x 21
```

18.
```
   52
 x 24
```

19.
```
   34
 x 12
```

20.
```
   14
 x 12
```

Practice 23 ⟳ ⟳ ⟳ ⟳ ⟳ ⟳ ⟳ ⟳ ⟳ ⟳ ⟳ ⟳ ⟳

Directions: Do these problems. Use your multiplication chart, if needed. The first one has been done for you.

1. 44
    x 21
    44
  + 880
    924

2. 68
    x 11

3. 99
    x 11

4. 14
    x 22

5. 33
    x 23

6. 13
    x 32

7. 91
    x 73

8. 72
    x 14

9. 73
    x 21

10. 41
    x 47

11. 71
    x 25

12. 43
    x 33

13. 14
    x 12

14. 15
    x 12

15. 23
    x 32

16. 42
    x 24

17. 62
    x 24

18. 82
    x 31

19. 71
    x 61

20. 13
    x 13

Practice 24

Directions: Do these problems. Use your multiplication chart, if needed.

1. 123 x 3	**2.** 214 x 2	**3.** 324 x 2	**4.** 232 x 3

5. 333 x 3	**6.** 641 x 2	**7.** 922 x 3	**8.** 832 x 3

Directions: Try these. Regroup, as shown, in number 9.

9. ¹¹ 435 x 3 1,305	**10.** 229 x 9	**11.** 564 x 4	**12.** 495 x 5

13. 892 x 5	**14.** 667 x 4	**15.** 739 x 7	**16.** 363 x 4

17. 299 x 6	**18.** 816 x 8	**19.** 765 x 8	**20.** 398 x 5

Practice 25

Directions: Do these problems. Use your multiplication chart, if needed. The first one has been done for you.

1.
   31
   452
   x 7
   3,164

2. 995
   x 6

3. 278
   x 2

4. 743
   x 4

5. 549
   x 7

6. 834
   x 7

7. 652
   x 9

8. 639
   x 5

9. 529
   x 8

10. 409
   x 3

11. 506
   x 4

12. 406
   x 7

13. 302
   x 5

14. 807
   x 9

15. 309
   x 5

16. 309
   x 6

17. 919
   x 9

18. 230
   x 7

19. 704
   x 9

20. 310
   x 9

Practice 26

Directions: Do these problems. Use your multiplication chart, if needed. The first one has been done for you.

1.
```
  11
 5132
x    5
25,660
```

2.
```
 6243
x   2
```

3.
```
 8761
x   4
```

4.
```
 3652
x   4
```

5.
```
 3491
x   8
```

6.
```
 4842
x   7
```

7.
```
 6766
x   3
```

8.
```
 1991
x   7
```

9.
```
 2864
x   9
```

10.
```
 3901
x   7
```

11.
```
 4009
x   7
```

12.
```
 6008
x   7
```

13.
```
 4881
x   8
```

14.
```
 8888
x   9
```

15.
```
 3811
x   3
```

16.
```
 2345
x   5
```

17.
```
 7009
x   4
```

18.
```
 6439
x   7
```

19.
```
 8031
x   6
```

20.
```
 4455
x   8
```

Practice 27 ⟳ ⟳ ⟳ ⟳ ⟳ ⟳ ⟳ ⟳ ⟳ ⟳ ⟳ ⟳ ⟳ ⟳

Directions: Do these problems. Use your multiplication chart, if needed. The first one has been done for you.

1.
$$
\begin{array}{r}
1 \\
3 \\
36 \\
\times 25 \\
\hline
180 \\
+720 \\
\hline
900
\end{array}
$$

2.
$$
\begin{array}{r}
74 \\
\times 38 \\
\hline
\end{array}
$$

3.
$$
\begin{array}{r}
97 \\
\times 45 \\
\hline
\end{array}
$$

4.
$$
\begin{array}{r}
42 \\
\times 56 \\
\hline
\end{array}
$$

5.
$$
\begin{array}{r}
93 \\
\times 34 \\
\hline
\end{array}
$$

6.
$$
\begin{array}{r}
44 \\
\times 58 \\
\hline
\end{array}
$$

7.
$$
\begin{array}{r}
74 \\
\times 28 \\
\hline
\end{array}
$$

8.
$$
\begin{array}{r}
72 \\
\times 46 \\
\hline
\end{array}
$$

9.
$$
\begin{array}{r}
67 \\
\times 89 \\
\hline
\end{array}
$$

10.
$$
\begin{array}{r}
85 \\
\times 63 \\
\hline
\end{array}
$$

11.
$$
\begin{array}{r}
58 \\
\times 36 \\
\hline
\end{array}
$$

12.
$$
\begin{array}{r}
92 \\
\times 54 \\
\hline
\end{array}
$$

13.
$$
\begin{array}{r}
49 \\
\times 67 \\
\hline
\end{array}
$$

14.
$$
\begin{array}{r}
66 \\
\times 49 \\
\hline
\end{array}
$$

15.
$$
\begin{array}{r}
89 \\
\times 73 \\
\hline
\end{array}
$$

16.
$$
\begin{array}{r}
42 \\
\times 65 \\
\hline
\end{array}
$$

17.
$$
\begin{array}{r}
88 \\
\times 22 \\
\hline
\end{array}
$$

18.
$$
\begin{array}{r}
44 \\
\times 33 \\
\hline
\end{array}
$$

19.
$$
\begin{array}{r}
77 \\
\times 99 \\
\hline
\end{array}
$$

20.
$$
\begin{array}{r}
55 \\
\times 55 \\
\hline
\end{array}
$$

Practice 28

Directions: Do these problems. Use your multiplication chart, if needed. The first one has been done for you.

1.
```
    4
    4
   87
 x 76
  522
+6090
6,612
```

2.
```
   43
 x 56
```

3.
```
   37
 x 62
```

4.
```
   23
 x 46
```

5.
```
   54
 x 71
```

6.
```
   99
 x 52
```

7.
```
   23
 x 56
```

8.
```
   87
 x 73
```

9.
```
   73
 x 34
```

10.
```
   43
 x 53
```

11.
```
   84
 x 66
```

12.
```
   19
 x 18
```

13.
```
   29
 x 43
```

14.
```
   74
 x 98
```

15.
```
   46
 x 52
```

16.
```
   63
 x 44
```

17.
```
   47
 x 33
```

18.
```
   75
 x 62
```

19.
```
   18
 x 76
```

20.
```
   25
 x 36
```

Practice 29 ๐ ๏ ๐ ๏ ๐ ๏ ๐ ๏ ๐ ๏ ๐ ๏ ๐ ๐ ๏

Directions: Do these problems. Use your multiplication chart, if needed.

1. 33 x 77	**2.** 44 x 88	**3.** 55 x 99	**4.** 66 x 22
5. 23 x 32	**6.** 34 x 43	**7.** 45 x 54	**8.** 56 x 65
9. 15 x 51	**10.** 16 x 61	**11.** 17 x 71	**12.** 18 x 81
13. 99 x 99	**14.** 98 x 98	**15.** 97 x 97	**16.** 96 x 96
17. 88 x 88	**18.** 87 x 78	**19.** 86 x 68	**20.** 85 x 58

#3321 Practice Makes Perfect: Multiplication

Practice 30

Directions: Do these problems. Use your multiplication chart, if needed. The first one has been done for you.

1.
```
      1
      1
    145
  x  22
    290
 + 2900
  3,190
```

2.
```
    225
  x  33
```

3.
```
    325
  x  15
```

4.
```
    434
  x  65
```

5.
```
    576
  x  72
```

6.
```
    667
  x  89
```

7.
```
    333
  x  59
```

8.
```
    555
  x  48
```

9.
```
    999
  x  73
```

10.
```
    974
  x  46
```

11.
```
    889
  x  75
```

12.
```
    771
  x  43
```

13.
```
    809
  x  48
```

14.
```
    907
  x  28
```

15.
```
    706
  x  76
```

Practice 31

Directions: Do these problems. Use your multiplication chart, if needed. The first one has been done for you. The second one has been started for you.

1.
```
    12
    11
   459
  x 32
   918
+ 13,770
 14,688
```

2.
```
   64
  975
  x 29
 8775
```

3.
```
  215
 x 62
```

4.
```
  818
 x 71
```

5.
```
  915
 x 49
```

6.
```
  714
 x 53
```

7.
```
  609
 x 72
```

8.
```
  906
 x 34
```

9.
```
  207
 x 39
```

10.
```
  900
 x 23
```

11.
```
  400
 x 63
```

12.
```
  600
 x 65
```

13.
```
  320
 x 78
```

14.
```
  780
 x 39
```

15.
```
  560
 x 49
```

Practice 32

Directions: Solve these problems. Use your multiplication chart, if needed.

1. What is the product of 34 and 20? _____

2. How much is 3 times 48? _____

3. Multiply 40 by 23. _____

4. Joanna has 31 pennies. George has 12 times as many pennies. How many pennies does George have? _____

5. Jennifer collected 17 posters. Her friend, Michelle, collected 10 times as many posters. How many posters did Michelle collect? _____

6. What is the product of 81 and 24? _____

7. What is 13 times 65? _____

8. Daniel has 44 trading cards. James has 13 times as many cards. How many cards does James have? _____

9. Compute the product of 35 and 23. _____

10. Multiply 45 and 67. _____

Practice 33

Directions: Solve these problems. Use your multiplication chart, if needed.

1. Compute the product of 5 and 43. _____

2. Multiply 16 times 36. _____

3. Crystal has 13 quarters in her piggy bank. Marissa has 11 times as many quarters. How many quarters does Marissa have? _____

4. What is the product of 34 and 43? _____

5. What is 40 times 84? _____

6. George has a collection of 9 CDs by his favorite artist. Each CD has 16 songs. How many songs altogether does George have on these CDs? _____

7. Name the product of 18 and 28. _____

8. What is 19 times 91? _____

9. Multiply 65 and 41. _____

10. Janice found 23 dimes under a sofa. She found 6 times as many pennies under the couch. How many pennies did she find? _____

Practice 34

The area of a rectangle is computed by multiplying the length times the width of the rectangle.

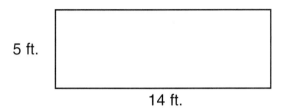

5 ft.

14 ft.

14 x 5 = 70 The area equals 70 square feet.

Directions: Calculate the area of these rectangles. The first one is started for you.

1.

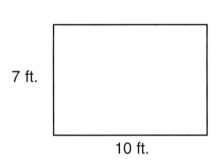

7 ft.

10 ft.

Area = 7 x 10 = _____ sq. ft.

2.

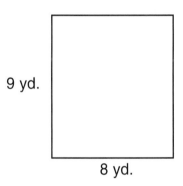

9 yd.

8 yd.

Area = _____ sq. yd.

3.

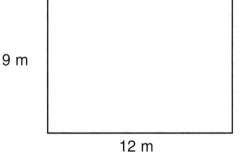

9 m

12 m

Area = _____ sq. m

4.

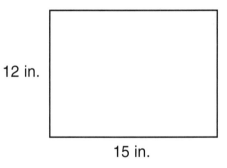

12 in.

15 in.

Area = _____ sq. in.

5.

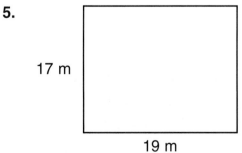

17 m

19 m

Area = _____ sq. m

6.

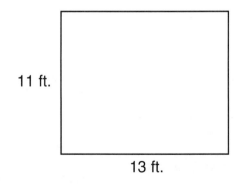

11 ft.

13 ft.

Area = _____ sq. ft.

Practice 35

Directions: Do these problems. Use your multiplication chart, if needed. The first one has been done for you.

1.
```
    2
  311
  6723
  x  35
  33615
+ 201690
 235,305
```

2.
```
  9534
  x  62
```

3.
```
  4321
  x  42
```

4.
```
  2233
  x  63
```

5.
```
  3332
  x  94
```

6.
```
  4554
  x  36
```

7.
```
  2197
  x  42
```

8.
```
  7642
  x  19
```

9.
```
  5623
  x  81
```

10.
```
  8701
  x  57
```

11.
```
  6740
  x  16
```

12.
```
  2905
  x  27
```

13.
```
  8998
  x  50
```

14.
```
  3355
  x  70
```

15.
```
  1122
  x  60
```

Practice 36

Directions: Do these problems. Use your multiplication chart, if needed. The first one is done for you.

1.   213
    x 412
      426
   2,130
 + 85,200
  87,756
	2. 423
	    x 263
		3. 523
		    x 326

4.   145
    x 218
	5. 229
	    x 612
		6. 196
		    x 513

7.   546
    x 623
	8. 498
	    x 252
		9. 654
		    x 548

Test Practice 1 ⟋ ❧ ⟋ ❧ ⟋ ❧ ⟋ ❧ ⟋ ❧ ⟋ ⟋ ❧

Directions: Solve each multiplication problem. On the Answer Sheet, fill in the answer circle for your choice.

1. 23
    x 9
    - Ⓐ 1,827
    - Ⓑ 187
    - Ⓒ 207
    - Ⓓ 217

2. 54
    x 7
    - Ⓐ 378
    - Ⓑ 3,528
    - Ⓒ 358
    - Ⓓ 498

3. 45
    x 7
    - Ⓐ 335
    - Ⓑ 2,835
    - Ⓒ 435
    - Ⓓ 315

4. 98
    x 6
    - Ⓐ 688
    - Ⓑ 5,648
    - Ⓒ 588
    - Ⓓ 598

5. 19
    x 9
    - Ⓐ 171
    - Ⓑ 981
    - Ⓒ 181
    - Ⓓ 271

6. 27
    x 8
    - Ⓐ 266
    - Ⓑ 216
    - Ⓒ 1,656
    - Ⓓ 415

7. 87
    x 9
    - Ⓐ 784
    - Ⓑ 773
    - Ⓒ 7,263
    - Ⓓ 783

8. 63 x 5 = _____
    - Ⓐ 315
    - Ⓑ 335
    - Ⓒ 3,015
    - Ⓓ 415

9. 94 x 7 = _____
    - Ⓐ 659
    - Ⓑ 658
    - Ⓒ 6,328
    - Ⓓ 668

10. 9 x 37 = _____
    - Ⓐ 333
    - Ⓑ 343
    - Ⓒ 2,763
    - Ⓓ 433

11. 6 x 17 = _____
    - Ⓐ 112
    - Ⓑ 102
    - Ⓒ 202
    - Ⓓ 642

12. 76 x 8 = _____
    - Ⓐ 688
    - Ⓑ 5,648
    - Ⓒ 618
    - Ⓓ 608

13. 38 x 9 = _____
    - Ⓐ 342
    - Ⓑ 2,772
    - Ⓒ 442
    - Ⓓ 352

14. 43 x 7 = _____
    - Ⓐ 311
    - Ⓑ 2,821
    - Ⓒ 2,721
    - Ⓓ 301

Test Practice 2

Directions: Solve each multiplication problem. On the Answer Sheet, fill in the answer circle for your choice.

1. $\begin{array}{r} 45 \\ \times\ 10 \end{array}$

    (A) 45
    (B) 405
    (C) 450
    (D) 4,500

2. $\begin{array}{r} 18 \\ \times\ 10 \end{array}$

    (A) 180
    (B) 1,800
    (C) 108
    (D) 188

3. $\begin{array}{r} 67 \\ \times\ 10 \end{array}$

    (A) 607
    (B) 6,107
    (C) 671
    (D) 670

4. $\begin{array}{r} 83 \\ \times\ 10 \end{array}$

    (A) 830
    (B) 8,310
    (C) 803
    (D) 831

5. $\begin{array}{r} 56 \\ \times\ 10 \end{array}$

    (A) 5,010
    (B) 506
    (C) 5,060
    (D) 560

6. $\begin{array}{r} 94 \\ \times\ 10 \end{array}$

    (A) 904
    (B) 940
    (C) 941
    (D) 9,410

7. $\begin{array}{r} 35 \\ \times\ 100 \end{array}$

    (A) 350
    (B) 3,500
    (C) 3,050
    (D) 3,150

8. 17 x 100 = _____

    (A) 170
    (B) 1,070
    (C) 1,700
    (D) 1,710

9. 94 x 100 = _____

    (A) 9,040
    (B) 9,400
    (C) 904
    (D) 9,004

10. 100 x 14 = _____

    (A) 1,410
    (B) 1,040
    (C) 140
    (D) 1,400

11. 100 x 26 = _____

    (A) 2,060
    (B) 260
    (C) 2,600
    (D) 2,610

12. 33 x 100 = _____

    (A) 330
    (B) 3,300
    (C) 3,030
    (D) 3,330

13. 43 x 100 = _____

    (A) 403
    (B) 4,310
    (C) 4,300
    (D) 4,030

14. 100 x 78 = _____

    (A) 7,800
    (B) 7,008
    (C) 7,810
    (D) 7,080

Test Practice 3

Directions: Solve each multiplication problem. On the Answer Sheet, fill in the answer circle for your choice.

1. 25
x 20
- Ⓐ 4,100
- Ⓑ 500
- Ⓒ 550
- Ⓓ 510

2. 41
x 30
- Ⓐ 1,240
- Ⓑ 430
- Ⓒ 1,230
- Ⓓ 700

3. 79
x 50
- Ⓐ 3,850
- Ⓑ 3,950
- Ⓒ 3,905
- Ⓓ 3,900

4. 29
x 30
- Ⓐ 880
- Ⓑ 6,110
- Ⓒ 870
- Ⓓ 740

5. 46
x 80
- Ⓐ 3,880
- Ⓑ 3,870
- Ⓒ 3,680
- Ⓓ 3,608

6. 98
x 70
- Ⓐ 6,860
- Ⓑ 6,660
- Ⓒ 9,560
- Ⓓ 7,860

7. 99
x 40
- Ⓐ 4,060
- Ⓑ 3,660
- Ⓒ 3,960
- Ⓓ 3,940

8. 78 x 90 = _____
- Ⓐ 7,220
- Ⓑ 7,020
- Ⓒ 7,200
- Ⓓ 7,720

9. 351 x 20 = _____
- Ⓐ 704
- Ⓑ 6,020
- Ⓒ 720
- Ⓓ 7,020

10. 469 x 30 = _____
- Ⓐ 1,470
- Ⓑ 14,770
- Ⓒ 1,740
- Ⓓ 14,070

11. 215 x 90 = _____
- Ⓐ 19,350
- Ⓑ 19,450
- Ⓒ 29,350
- Ⓓ 19,360

12. 674 x 70 = _____
- Ⓐ 47,280
- Ⓑ 47,190
- Ⓒ 47,180
- Ⓓ 48,180

13. 3124 x 20 = _____
- Ⓐ 63,480
- Ⓑ 62,490
- Ⓒ 62,480
- Ⓓ 62,880

14. 2995 x 50 = _____
- Ⓐ 149,750
- Ⓑ 148,850
- Ⓒ 14,975
- Ⓓ 150,750

Test Practice 4 ⟳ ⟲ ⟳ ⟲ ⟳ ⟲ ⟳ ⟲ ⟳ ⟳ ⟲

Directions: Solve each multiplication problem. On the Answer Sheet, fill in the answer circle for your choice.

1. 45
    x 10
    - (A) 322
    - (B) 450
    - (C) 3,264
    - (D) 394

2. 44
    x 22
    - (A) 968
    - (B) 8,888
    - (C) 288
    - (D) 988

3. 13
    x 33
    - (A) 439
    - (B) 1,333
    - (C) 429
    - (D) 329

4. 23
    x 23
    - (A) 549
    - (B) 529
    - (C) 263
    - (D) 439

5. 89
    x 15
    - (A) 1,355
    - (B) 1,895
    - (C) 2,335
    - (D) 1,335

6. 45
    x 73
    - (A) 3,285
    - (B) 3,295
    - (C) 4,123
    - (D) 4,285

7. 78
    x 54
    - (A) 4,214
    - (B) 5,212
    - (C) 4,312
    - (D) 4,212

8. 91 x 65 = _____
    - (A) 5,915
    - (B) 5,925
    - (C) 5,415
    - (D) 5,935

9. 89 x 32 = _____
    - (A) 2,868
    - (B) 2,948
    - (C) 3,048
    - (D) 2,848

10. 44 x 66 = _____
    - (A) 3,904
    - (B) 2,914
    - (C) 2,984
    - (D) 2,904

11. 25 x 25 = _____
    - (A) 6,225
    - (B) 625
    - (C) 675
    - (D) 425

12. 99 x 29 = _____
    - (A) 2,891
    - (B) 2,971
    - (C) 2,871
    - (D) 3,871

13. 26 x 62 = _____
    - (A) 362
    - (B) 1,632
    - (C) 1,602
    - (D) 1,612

14. 41 x 14 = _____
    - (A) 4,114
    - (B) 574
    - (C) 594
    - (D) 674

Test Practice 5 ꙮ ꙮ ꙮ ꙮ ꙮ ꙮ ꙮ ꙮ ꙮ ꙮ ꙮ

Directions: Solve each multiplication problem. On the Answer Sheet, fill in the answer circle for your choice.

1. 49
   x 34
   - (A) 1,686
   - (B) 2,666
   - (C) 1,666
   - (D) 1,696

8. 18 x 81 = _____
   - (A) 1,438
   - (B) 1,448
   - (C) 1,558
   - (D) 1,458

2. 77
   x 27
   - (A) 2,079
   - (B) 2,179
   - (C) 2,169
   - (D) 2,069

9. 17 x 28 = _____
   - (A) 476
   - (B) 576
   - (C) 4,076
   - (D) 478

3. 88
   x 37
   - (A) 3,266
   - (B) 3,356
   - (C) 3,156
   - (D) 3,256

10. 66 x 67 = _____
    - (A) 4,322
    - (B) 4,422
    - (C) 4,412
    - (D) 4,432

4. 19
   x 92
   - (A) 2,748
   - (B) 1,758
   - (C) 1,748
   - (D) 7,148

11. 19 x 57 = _____
    - (A) 1,183
    - (B) 993
    - (C) 1,193
    - (D) 1,083

5. 87
   x 55
   - (A) 4,885
   - (B) 4,785
   - (C) 4,795
   - (D) 4,985

12. 23 x 39 = _____
    - (A) 997
    - (B) 987
    - (C) 897
    - (D) 1,087

6. 39
   x 17
   - (A) 1,663
   - (B) 663
   - (C) 636
   - (D) 693

13. 47 x 26 = _____
    - (A) 1,222
    - (B) 1,232
    - (C) 2,222
    - (D) 3,222

7. 94
   x 49
   - (A) 4,616
   - (B) 6,606
   - (C) 4,606
   - (D) 4,660

14. 24 x 48 = _____
    - (A) 1,154
    - (B) 1,352
    - (C) 1,152
    - (D) 1,252

Test Practice 6

Directions: Solve each multiplication problem. On the Answer Sheet, fill in the answer circle for your choice.

1. 321
    x 22

    Ⓐ 7,162
    Ⓑ 7,052
    Ⓒ 7,062
    Ⓓ 6,962

2. 251
    x 13

    Ⓐ 3,263
    Ⓑ 3,363
    Ⓒ 3,353
    Ⓓ 3,063

3. 529
    x 11

    Ⓐ 5,918
    Ⓑ 5,891
    Ⓒ 5,819
    Ⓓ 6,819

4. 698
    x 24

    Ⓐ 16,742
    Ⓑ 16,752
    Ⓒ 16,725
    Ⓓ 16,652

5. 728
    x 43

    Ⓐ 31,340
    Ⓑ 32,304
    Ⓒ 33,304
    Ⓓ 31,304

6. 999
    x 99

    Ⓐ 98,909
    Ⓑ 98,109
    Ⓒ 98,901
    Ⓓ 99,999

7. 4,516
    x 31

    Ⓐ 139,999
    Ⓑ 139,906
    Ⓒ 138,996
    Ⓓ 139,996

8. 5,613
    x 33

    Ⓐ 185,229
    Ⓑ 185,239
    Ⓒ 186,229
    Ⓓ 186,229

9. 536
    x 498

    Ⓐ 267,928
    Ⓑ 266,938
    Ⓒ 266,908
    Ⓓ 266,928

10. 602
    x 507

    Ⓐ 315,214
    Ⓑ 305,214
    Ⓒ 325,214
    Ⓓ 305,224

11. 979
    x 746

    Ⓐ 730,344
    Ⓑ 731,334
    Ⓒ 730,334
    Ⓓ 733,334

12. 398
    x 610

    Ⓐ 242,780
    Ⓑ 244,780
    Ⓒ 442,780
    Ⓓ 242,708

Answer Sheet

Test Practice 1	Test Practice 2	Test Practice 3
1. Ⓐ Ⓑ Ⓒ Ⓓ	1. Ⓐ Ⓑ Ⓒ Ⓓ	1. Ⓐ Ⓑ Ⓒ Ⓓ
2. Ⓐ Ⓑ Ⓒ Ⓓ	2. Ⓐ Ⓑ Ⓒ Ⓓ	2. Ⓐ Ⓑ Ⓒ Ⓓ
3. Ⓐ Ⓑ Ⓒ Ⓓ	3. Ⓐ Ⓑ Ⓒ Ⓓ	3. Ⓐ Ⓑ Ⓒ Ⓓ
4. Ⓐ Ⓑ Ⓒ Ⓓ	4. Ⓐ Ⓑ Ⓒ Ⓓ	4. Ⓐ Ⓑ Ⓒ Ⓓ
5. Ⓐ Ⓑ Ⓒ Ⓓ	5. Ⓐ Ⓑ Ⓒ Ⓓ	5. Ⓐ Ⓑ Ⓒ Ⓓ
6. Ⓐ Ⓑ Ⓒ Ⓓ	6. Ⓐ Ⓑ Ⓒ Ⓓ	6. Ⓐ Ⓑ Ⓒ Ⓓ
7. Ⓐ Ⓑ Ⓒ Ⓓ	7. Ⓐ Ⓑ Ⓒ Ⓓ	7. Ⓐ Ⓑ Ⓒ Ⓓ
8. Ⓐ Ⓑ Ⓒ Ⓓ	8. Ⓐ Ⓑ Ⓒ Ⓓ	8. Ⓐ Ⓑ Ⓒ Ⓓ
9. Ⓐ Ⓑ Ⓒ Ⓓ	9. Ⓐ Ⓑ Ⓒ Ⓓ	9. Ⓐ Ⓑ Ⓒ Ⓓ
10. Ⓐ Ⓑ Ⓒ Ⓓ	10. Ⓐ Ⓑ Ⓒ Ⓓ	10. Ⓐ Ⓑ Ⓒ Ⓓ
11. Ⓐ Ⓑ Ⓒ Ⓓ	11. Ⓐ Ⓑ Ⓒ Ⓓ	11. Ⓐ Ⓑ Ⓒ Ⓓ
12. Ⓐ Ⓑ Ⓒ Ⓓ	12. Ⓐ Ⓑ Ⓒ Ⓓ	12. Ⓐ Ⓑ Ⓒ Ⓓ
13. Ⓐ Ⓑ Ⓒ Ⓓ	13. Ⓐ Ⓑ Ⓒ Ⓓ	13. Ⓐ Ⓑ Ⓒ Ⓓ
14. Ⓐ Ⓑ Ⓒ Ⓓ	14. Ⓐ Ⓑ Ⓒ Ⓓ	14. Ⓐ Ⓑ Ⓒ Ⓓ

Test Practice 4	Test Practice 5	Test Practice 6
1. Ⓐ Ⓑ Ⓒ Ⓓ	1. Ⓐ Ⓑ Ⓒ Ⓓ	1. Ⓐ Ⓑ Ⓒ Ⓓ
2. Ⓐ Ⓑ Ⓒ Ⓓ	2. Ⓐ Ⓑ Ⓒ Ⓓ	2. Ⓐ Ⓑ Ⓒ Ⓓ
3. Ⓐ Ⓑ Ⓒ Ⓓ	3. Ⓐ Ⓑ Ⓒ Ⓓ	3. Ⓐ Ⓑ Ⓒ Ⓓ
4. Ⓐ Ⓑ Ⓒ Ⓓ	4. Ⓐ Ⓑ Ⓒ Ⓓ	4. Ⓐ Ⓑ Ⓒ Ⓓ
5. Ⓐ Ⓑ Ⓒ Ⓓ	5. Ⓐ Ⓑ Ⓒ Ⓓ	5. Ⓐ Ⓑ Ⓒ Ⓓ
6. Ⓐ Ⓑ Ⓒ Ⓓ	6. Ⓐ Ⓑ Ⓒ Ⓓ	6. Ⓐ Ⓑ Ⓒ Ⓓ
7. Ⓐ Ⓑ Ⓒ Ⓓ	7. Ⓐ Ⓑ Ⓒ Ⓓ	7. Ⓐ Ⓑ Ⓒ Ⓓ
8. Ⓐ Ⓑ Ⓒ Ⓓ	8. Ⓐ Ⓑ Ⓒ Ⓓ	8. Ⓐ Ⓑ Ⓒ Ⓓ
9. Ⓐ Ⓑ Ⓒ Ⓓ	9. Ⓐ Ⓑ Ⓒ Ⓓ	9. Ⓐ Ⓑ Ⓒ Ⓓ
10. Ⓐ Ⓑ Ⓒ Ⓓ	10. Ⓐ Ⓑ Ⓒ Ⓓ	10. Ⓐ Ⓑ Ⓒ Ⓓ
11. Ⓐ Ⓑ Ⓒ Ⓓ	11. Ⓐ Ⓑ Ⓒ Ⓓ	11. Ⓐ Ⓑ Ⓒ Ⓓ
12. Ⓐ Ⓑ Ⓒ Ⓓ	12. Ⓐ Ⓑ Ⓒ Ⓓ	12. Ⓐ Ⓑ Ⓒ Ⓓ
13. Ⓐ Ⓑ Ⓒ Ⓓ	13. Ⓐ Ⓑ Ⓒ Ⓓ	
14. Ⓐ Ⓑ Ⓒ Ⓓ	14. Ⓐ Ⓑ Ⓒ Ⓓ	

Answer Key

Page 4
1. 63
2. 20
3. 27
4. 12
5. 16
6. 25
7. 36
8. 9

Page 5
1. 15
2. 12
3. 8
4. 24
5. 24
6. 36
7. 10
8. 18
9. 7
10. 35
11. 20
12. 15
13. 30
14. 30
15. 27
16. 32

Page 6
1. 1
2. 4
3. 10
4. 0
5. 10
6. 2
7. 0
8. 0
9. 0
10. 5
11. 0
12. 2
13. 6
14. 7
15. 9
16. 8
17. 0
18. 0
19. 0
20. 0
21. 18
22. 12
23. 14
24. 8
25. 35

Page 7
1. 9
2. 10
3. 18
4. 0
5. 16
6. 30
7. 9
8. 30
9. 40
10. 10
11. 0
12. 8
13. 14
14. 7
15. 20

16. 0
17. 0
18. 50
19. 0
20. 0
21. 20
22. 30
23. 40
24. 45
25. 0

Page 8
1. 20
2. 8
3. 30
4. 3
5. 7
6. 21
7. 30
8. 0
9. 5
10. 9
11. 18
12. 0
13. 40
14. 27
15. 4
16. 24
17. 50
18. 36
19. 12
20. 18
21. 21
22. 6
23. 30
24. 14
25. 16

Page 9
1. 24
2. 16
3. 32
4. 40
5. 35
6. 7
7. 70
8. 28
9. 12
10. 24
11. 18
12. 30
13. 45
14. 0
15. 18
16. 9
17. 18
18. 40
19. 60
20. 42
21. 30
22. 72
23. 63
24. 54
25. 49

Page 10
1. 36
2. 42
3. 16
4. 0
5. 35

6. 72
7. 56
8. 6
9. 24
10. 40
11. 20
12. 24
13. 45
14. 64
15. 90
16. 40
17. 21
18. 63
19. 56
20. 48
21. 40
22. 90
23. 70
24. 6
25. 80

Page 11
1. 72
2. 36
3. 63
4. 60
5. 40
6. 0
7. 27
8. 7
9. 49
10. 30
11. 54
12. 56
13. 63
14. 45
15. 35
16. 28
17. 0
18. 18
19. 32
20. 6
21. 48
22. 10
23. 0
24. 72
25. 28

Page 12
1. 5
2. 2
3. 4
4. 8
5. 10
6. 5
7. 6
8. 4
9. 10
10. 6
11. 9
12. 3
13. 9
14. 7
15. 6
16. 8
17. 4
18. 8
19. 9
20. 4
21. 10

22. 7
23. 6
24. 9
25. 7
26. 8
27. 4

Page 13
1. 110
2. 120
3. 96
4. 132
5. 99
6. 33
7. 99
8. 72
9. 120
10. 108
11. 66
12. 48
13. 108
14. 88
15. 60
16. 77
17. 36
18. 132
19. 84
20. 48
21. 88
22. 55
23. 36
24. 96
25. 108

Page 14
1. 24
2. 24
3. 24
4. 36
5. 36
6. 36
7. 120
8. 120
9. 120
10. 105
11. 105
12. 105
13. 72
14. 72
15. 72

Page 15
1. 48
2. 28
3. 39
4. 63
5. 126
6. 88
7. 88
8. 68
9. 400
10. 168
11. 108
12. 86
13. 99
14. 639
15. 67
16. 279
17. 90
18. 170
19. 140

20. 260
21. 630
22. 630
23. 300
24. 480
25. 160

Page 16
1. 99
2. 30
3. 69
4. 246
5. 255
6. 68
7. 75
8. 128
9. 125
10. 69
11. 48
12. 110
13. 90
14. 135
15. 180
16. 108
17. 220
18. 264
19. 132
20. 220
21. 204
22. 148
23. 112
24. 325
25. 208

Page 17
1. 252
2. 450
3. 651
4. 282
5. 295
6. 760
7. 435
8. 237
9. 595
10. 511
11. 603
12. 368
13. 702
14. 792
15. 686
16. 456
17. 231
18. 57
19. 392
20. 657
21. 522
22. 222
23. 648
24. 232
25. 608

Page 18
1. 120
2. 150
3. 230
4. 110
5. 220
6. 140
7. 330
8. 180
9. 200

10. 400
11. 300
12. 700
13. 240
14. 310
15. 620
16. 430
17. 440
18. 250
19. 370
20. 620

Page 19
1. 640
2. 1,000
3. 390
4. 320
5. 450
6. 3,680
7. 850
8. 1,680
9. 690
10. 3,360
11. 1,440
12. 1,700
13. 420
14. 990
15. 2,160
16. 1,680
17. 2,750
18. 8,910
19. 990
20. 3,960

Page 20
1. 1,230
2. 5,430
3. 2,430
4. 3,410
5. 2,440
6. 5,340
7. 3,330
8. 7,620
9. 3,000
10. 4,000
11. 7,000
12. 9,000
13. 2,500
14. 4,600
15. 6,200
16. 4,900
17. 4,740
18. 7,160
19. 6,420
20. 9,190

Page 21
1. 2,680
2. 35,550
3. 3,690
4. 5,800
5. 3,750
6. 6,840
7. 13,880
8. 8,840
9. 9,990
10. 17,760
11. 4,440
12. 9,990
13. 36,550
14. 54,360

Answer Key

15. 65,800
16. 33,040
17. 49,000
18. 20,000
19. 56,000
20. 24,000

Page 22
1. 6,000
2. 6,000
3. 24,000
4. 14,000
5. 60,000
6. 60,000
7. 144,000
8. 224,000
9. 216,000
10. 64,000
11. 504,000
12. 48,000

Page 23
1. 2,300
2. 4,500
3. 1,900
4. 1,200
5. 4,200
6. 8,700
7. 3,300
8. 2,900
9. 40,000
10. 60,000
11. 30,000
12. 80,000
13. 71,200
14. 45,600
15. 81,700
16. 11,100
17. 43,800
18. 12,500
19. 98,200
20. 81,900

Page 24
1. 14,000
2. 21,000
3. 17,000
4. 28,000
5. 75,000
6. 33,000
7. 219,000
8. 495,000
9. 239,000
10. 200,000
11. 500,000
12. 400,000
13. 2,345,000
14. 6,126,000
15. 4,949,000
16. 3,498,000

Page 25
1. 252
2. 308
3. 276
4. 744
5. 286
6. 748
7. 704
8. 429
9. 1,140

10. 1,720
11. 4,402
12. 1,333
13. 726
14. 1,763
15. 748
16. 736
17. 924
18. 1,248
19. 408
20. 168

Page 26
1. 924
2. 748
3. 1,089
4. 308
5. 759
6. 416
7. 6,643
8. 1,008
9. 1,533
10. 1,927
11. 1,775
12. 1,419
13. 168
14. 180
15. 736
16. 1,008
17. 1,488
18. 2,542
19. 4,331
20. 169

Page 27
1. 369
2. 428
3. 648
4. 696
5. 999
6. 1,282
7. 2,766
8. 2,496
9. 1,305
10. 2,061
11. 2,256
12. 2,475
13. 4,460
14. 2,668
15. 5,173
16. 1,452
17. 1,794
18. 6,528
19. 6,120
20. 1,990

Page 28
1. 3,164
2. 5,970
3. 556
4. 2,972
5. 3,843
6. 5,838
7. 5,868
8. 3,195
9. 4,232
10. 1,227
11. 2,024
12. 2,842
13. 1,510
14. 7,263

15. 1,545
16. 1,854
17. 8,271
18. 1,610
19. 6,336
20. 2,790

Page 29
1. 25,660
2. 12,486
3. 35,044
4. 14,608
5. 27,928
6. 33,894
7. 20,298
8. 13,937
9. 25,776
10. 27,307
11. 28,063
12. 42,056
13. 39,048
14. 79,992
15. 11,433
16. 11,725
17. 28,036
18. 45,073
19. 48,186
20. 35,640

Page 30
1. 900
2. 2,812
3. 4,365
4. 2,352
5. 3,162
6. 2,552
7. 2,072
8. 3,312
9. 5,963
10. 5,355
11. 2,088
12. 4,968
13. 3,283
14. 3,234
15. 6,497
16. 2,730
17. 1,936
18. 1,452
19. 7,623
20. 3,025

Page 31
1. 6,612
2. 2,408
3. 2,294
4. 1,058
5. 3,834
6. 5,148
7. 1,288
8. 6,351
9. 2,482
10. 2,279
11. 5,544
12. 342
13. 1,247
14. 7,252
15. 2,392
16. 2,772
17. 1,551
18. 4,650
19. 1,368

20. 900

Page 32
1. 2,541
2. 3,872
3. 5,445
4. 1,452
5. 736
6. 1,462
7. 2,430
8. 3,640
9. 765
10. 976
11. 1,207
12. 1,458
13. 9,801
14. 9,604
15. 9,409
16. 9,216
17. 7,744
18. 6,786
19. 5,848
20. 4,930

Page 33
1. 3,190
2. 7,425
3. 4,875
4. 28,210
5. 41,472
6. 59,363
7. 19,647
8. 26,640
9. 72,927
10. 44,804
11. 66,675
12. 33,153
13. 38,832
14. 25,396
15. 53,656

Page 34
1. 14,688
2. 28,275
3. 13,330
4. 58,078
5. 44,835
6. 37,842
7. 43,848
8. 30,804
9. 8,073
10. 20,700
11. 25,200
12. 39,000
13. 24,960
14. 30,420
15. 27,440

Page 35
1. 680
2. 144
3. 920
4. 372 pennies
5. 170 posters
6. 1,944
7. 845
8. 572 cards
9. 805
10. 3,015

Page 36
1. 215

2. 576
3. 143 quarters
4. 1,462
5. 3,360
6. 144 songs
7. 504
8. 1,729
9. 2,665
10. 138 pennies

Page 37
1. 70 sq. ft.
2. 72 sq. yd.
3. 108 sq. m
4. 180 sq. in.
5. 323 sq. m
6. 143 sq. ft.

Page 38
1. 235,305
2. 591,108
3. 181,482
4. 140,679
5. 313,208
6. 163,944
7. 92,274
8. 145,198
9. 455,463
10. 495,957
11. 107,840
12. 78,435
13. 449,900
14. 234,850
15. 67,320

Page 39
1. 87,756
2. 111,249
3. 170,498
4. 31,610
5. 140,148
6. 100,548
7. 340,158
8. 125,496
9. 358,392

Page 40
1. C
2. A
3. D
4. C
5. A
6. B
7. D
8. A
9. B
10. A
11. B
12. D
13. A
14. D

Page 41
1. C
2. A
3. D
4. A
5. D
6. B
7. B
8. C
9. B

10. D
11. C
12. B
13. C
14. A

Page 42
1. B
2. C
3. B
4. C
5. C
6. A
7. C
8. B
9. D
10. D
11. A
12. C
13. C
14. A

Page 43
1. B
2. A
3. C
4. B
5. D
6. A
7. D
8. A
9. D
10. D
11. B
12. C
13. D
14. B

Page 44
1. C
2. A
3. D
4. C
5. B
6. B
7. C
8. D
9. A
10. B
11. D
12. C
13. A
14. C

Page 45
1. C
2. A
3. C
4. B
5. D
6. C
7. D
8. A
9. D
10. B
11. C
12. A